HOW TO HEAL
EMOTIONAL TRAUMA

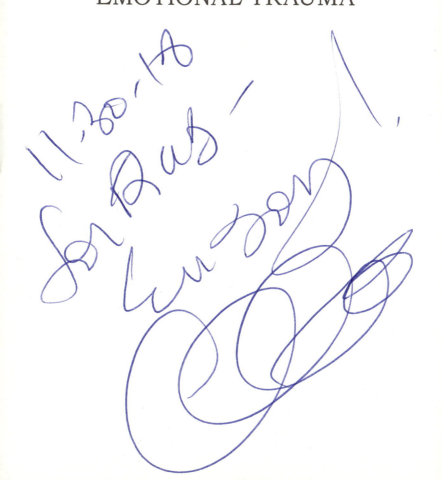

HOW TO HEAL EMOTIONAL TRAUMA

7 KEYS TO FINDING FREEDOM AND SELF-WORTH

DR. ANITA GADHIA-SMITH

HOW TO HEAL EMOTIONAL TRAUMA
7 KEYS TO FINDING FREEDOM AND SELF-WORTH

Copyright © 2018 DR. ANITA GADHIA-SMITH.

All rights reserved. No part of this book may be used or reproduced by any means, graphic, electronic, or mechanical, including photocopying, recording, taping or by any information storage retrieval system without the written permission of the author except in the case of brief quotations embodied in critical articles and reviews.

iUniverse books may be ordered through booksellers or by contacting:

iUniverse
1663 Liberty Drive
Bloomington, IN 47403
www.iuniverse.com
1-800-Authors (1-800-288-4677)

Because of the dynamic nature of the Internet, any web addresses or links contained in this book may have changed since publication and may no longer be valid. The views expressed in this work are solely those of the author and do not necessarily reflect the views of the publisher, and the publisher hereby disclaims any responsibility for them.

Any people depicted in stock imagery provided by Getty Images are models, and such images are being used for illustrative purposes only. Certain stock imagery © Getty Images.

ISBN: 978-1-5320-5836-3 (sc)
ISBN: 978-1-5320-5837-0 (e)

Print information available on the last page.

iUniverse rev. date: 09/19/2018

CONTENTS

FOREWORD ix

Chapter 1 COMING OUT OF DENIAL 1
Chapter 2 WHERE ARE THE
           FEELINGS NOW? 11
Chapter 3 IDENTIFY BEHAVIOR
           PATTERNS 23
Chapter 4 IDENTIFY BELIEFS 39
Chapter 5 STOP ACCEPTING
           ABUSE AND SELF-
           SABOTAGE 57
Chapter 6 LETTING GO OF THE
           VICTIM MENTALITY 75
Chapter 7 DEVELOPING
           SELF WORTH........................85

ABOUT THE AUTHOR........................... 123

**THIS BOOK IS DEDICATED
TO MY PATIENTS**

FOREWORD

Life is difficult, and can be filled with loss, suffering, regret, and painful memories. The pain inflicted by nature, the loss of loved ones, economic disasters, and medical illnesses are part of the journey and seldom can the individual change these outcomes.

But there are other forms of suffering, more common and universal. Perhaps the most difficult pains to bear are those psychic pains, caused not by ourselves or nature, but inflicted upon us by others through indifference, malice, or a carelessness born of narcissism.

Dr. Gadhia Smith's long interest, observation, care, and treatment of those individuals suffering from pain inflicted, often by loved ones, close friends, and employers, has enabled her to develop an expertise I have not seen in other therapists. In this remarkable book, she writes with clarity and an active, joyous approach to empower the reader to live a life of action, purpose and direct effective confrontation of their issues.

In these pages Dr. Gadhia Smith teaches the importance of acknowledging the reality and origin of recurrent psychic suffering, of putting the pain into words, of having the pain witnessed by others, and doing the hard work to forgive, avoid recurrence, and get free.

This book allows those wishing to recover from emotional pain to develop a capacity to deal with universal suffering. Read this book with an open mind and willingness to take action in order to get free, and live and love without oppression from recurrent wounds.

"There is, in all of us, a great unhealed place"
Lawrence Durrell

RONALD EARL SMITH, MD, PHD
CAPTAIN, (RET), MEDICAL CORPS
UNITED STATES NAVY

1
COMING OUT OF DENIAL

The first step in the healing process is to recognize that you have experienced emotional trauma, and the effects of it are real. Many of us are not aware that we have experienced emotional abuse and trauma. Trauma can be stored deep inside of us for a long time, and we may not be in touch with it. When you have experienced or grown up with toxic, harmful relationships, there is a tendency to become desensitized to its effects and replicate these dynamics in your other relationships.

Most of this happens at the unconscious level, so we don't know what we're doing. We are drawn to the familiar, even though it might not be good for us, because it is more comfortable than change. Change begins with new awareness, and as we start to become more conscious of our thoughts and actions, we can examine our deeper, inner driving forces and repetitive dynamics and create meaningful and lasting change in our lives.

The truth might not be hopeful, but telling it is. Someone else has gone through what you have. There is something about speaking your truth that is freeing for you and others. Although the content can be sad, the very act of speaking the truth is an action of hope and faith. No matter what your situation is, bringing it out into the light of day will help you, and you will discover that you are not alone.

By honoring your story, you can have hope that you are going to achieve freedom from the past. The only way through it is through it. You can't go around it, underneath it, or over it - you need to deal with your feelings in order to get to the other side. Once you realize that there is real hope for change, it is well worth the pain of talking about what happened to you.

This is not something that most would like to do, but it is something that most of us need to do in order to live fully and experience all of the joy and freedom that life can offer. You are not alone. Most of us have experienced difficulty in some form or another in our lives.

I don't know anyone who is immune from the pains of growing up, living, and having relationships with other human beings. Some of us are taught to deal with pain and adversity more effectively than others. If you were lucky enough to come from a highly functional and healthy family, you may have learned how to relate to people well and to do your inner work along the way. But for most of us, this is not the case. We need to take responsibility for our unresolved issues as adults and learn how to deal with them so that they do not control us. There is no quick fix, but healing happens when we work for it.

You are not defective, helpless, or alone.

You are not broken; you are just hurt, and you can heal. Just because you experienced trauma in your life does not mean that you cannot recover. It simply means that you have had painful experiences that have wounded you. Human beings are incredibly resilient, and there is a driving force within us to grow, repair, and heal. Once you understand that even your deepest wounds can and will heal, it will be much easier to decide to undertake the work you need to do. You must recognize it is time to face whatever has happened to you. The pain of the past will not go away by itself, so you might as well face it so that you can become free from its effects.

Most psychological work comes in layers and cycles. As one issue begins to surface, we work through that layer of our feelings. Each layer can take time, and we may experience a plateau for a while after we have done some significant work. This is the psyche's way of giving us a rest in the same way that we rest in each of our days in order to function well. We all go through naturally recurring cycles of activity and rest. We cannot do meaningful emotional work without taking some breaks to recharge.

As time goes on, we can continue to address layer after layer as we continue in our process of growth. With each successive layer, we go deeper. Some emotions have been buried so deeply that it can take decades of psychological work to access them, feel them, and process them. This tends to happen in a gentle and natural way, so that we are never required to do psychological surgery at a harmful pace. Rather, we are gently guided to whatever we need to do at the time we're supposed to.

We can never force something to happen before its time, and we can never stop something from happening when its time has come. We can trust that we are continuing to evolve and grow over time and that our growth will never stop if we remain engaged in the process. As we grow older and go through the aging process, we can continue to evolve into better versions of ourselves.

The most important ingredient in this ever-evolving growth process is honesty. This can be a challenge for some of us who are taught that the most important thing in life is to look good. In many dysfunctional relationships, the emphasis is on looking like you are well put together rather than functioning in a healthy way on the inside. Dysfunctional families believe that if you look okay, you are okay. When honesty becomes more important than looking good, you have made a significant step.

Many of us know that we are not really okay, and we have known that for a long time deep down inside. We go to great lengths to try to cover that up and hide what's really going on. We don't want anyone to know who we really are, because we are afraid that if they truly know us, they will reject us. Thus, we remain invested in creating, preserving, and presenting a false self to the world. We believe that this is what we're supposed to do and that this is what people want from us. We have been told that this will make us successful and get us what we want from others.

One way to know if you have unhealed trauma is if you continue to experience recurring intense emotional pain that won't go away. When you experience something painful that comes up over and over again, there is a deeper reason for it. It is not a coincidence, and it is not because you are weak or overly sensitive. If you find yourself becoming disproportionately distressed in situations, and it doesn't make sense to you, there is something to unpack from your history. It could be from early life experience or from your adult history. Some trauma occurs early in life, and other trauma occurs when we are adults as the result of toxic relationships. Whatever the cause, if it is hysterical, it is historical. Your emotional pain is telling you something important that you need to know. It is a call to action.

Some of us blame ourselves for the pain that we feel inside. We feel that it is our own fault and that we feel this pain because there is something wrong with us. We might think that we are defective in some way. We look at other people and think that they are happy and have it all together, and we do not. We feel inferior, as though we are not as good as they are. We blame ourselves for our shortcomings, and we carry a vague sense that there will always be something wrong with us no matter how much we accomplish. This can lead to getting caught the compulsive need to prove that we are okay. If we blame ourselves, then we think that the only solution is to try to fix ourselves. But until we attend to the deeper pain within, we will get caught in the trap of trying to fix only our externals and feeling like we never really have.

The trauma you've experienced isn't your fault, so stop blaming yourself. Once you realize that you did not cause your own trauma, even if someone else tells you that you did, you will experience a new sense of freedom. What happened to you was the result of someone else's dysfunction. They didn't know how to handle their own pain, so they took it out on you and transferred it to you. Because you didn't know what was happening, you didn't know how to protect yourself. You can't blame yourself for something that you didn't create, because the cause of what was done to you was much bigger than you.

In many cases, trauma is an intergenerational behavioral phenomenon that was passed down from family member to family member in generations that preceded yours. It could also have been a person outside of your family system who traumatized you. They may have experienced trauma themselves and dumped it onto you. Hurt people hurt people.

Much of the abuse that people inflict upon others is unintentional. In some cases, it is on purpose, but most people are simply acting out their pain onto others or reincarnating their own life experiences. They simply don't know how to handle whatever has happened to them, and they just do whatever they can to get through life. They are trying to survive and remain somewhat comfortable in their own skin. They are not out to get you. They just act, and they are not necessarily doing it to you on purpose.

You don't have to accept blame for the emotional trauma you have experienced. If you can honestly recognize what has happened to you and accept responsibility for dealing with it, you have already taken the most significant step in setting yourself free from the pain and reclaiming your self-worth. You have the power to seek help for yourself, heal from trauma, and create profound and lasting change in your inner being.

2

WHERE ARE THE FEELINGS NOW?

Feelings have a life span: a beginning, a middle, and an end. When something happens in our lives that creates an emotional reaction, feelings will happen, whether we want them to or not. If we are emotionally healthy, we will recognize that we are experiencing feelings, know what they are, name them, and claim them. Then we will be able to process them in an appropriate way. Sometimes this simply means recognizing them and letting them pass. Other times we need to address them before they will subside. For example, we may need to talk them out with someone, write about them, pray about them, or engage in physical activity.

In healthy families, we learn through observation how to handle feelings in an appropriate way. We learn that it is human to have feelings and that it is okay to talk about them. When we see the adults in our lives handling feelings in an honest and open way, we do the same. However, in dysfunctional families, feelings are often not acknowledged and are dismissed, minimized, or ignored. In the dysfunctional family system, there is often emotional denial, which results in feelings being repressed and buried deep within. When this occurs, especially over a long period, the feelings layer and build up. When you accumulate unprocessed feelings, they just stay inside you until you deal with them. They can remain buried inside of you for decades, or even a lifetime, and eventually become unconscious forces that control you until you deal with them.

Unprocessed feelings come out at inappropriate times when you don't want them to. An example of this is a situation where you have an extremely out of proportion reaction to a seemingly insignificant event. Something small happens, and you completely lose it. It can catch everyone off guard, especially the blindsided recipient of your feelings. When it is hysterical, it is often historical.

You may think that you are reacting to something that is happening in the present, but you have been triggered back into old feelings that never got processed. They can be so intense that you have no idea why you are doing what you are doing. For the unsuspecting person or people around you, it can be quite devastating and damaging to your relationships.

This is often how intense conflicts erupt spontaneously and take on a life of their own. Many individuals and couples that I have worked with over the years will report that they don't know how their fights started, and they can't even remember what they were about. "It just got crazy, and we didn't even know how we got there!" All they know is that suddenly they were in hell. It might take hours, or even sometimes days or weeks, to get out of it. When this type of emotional storm occurs, it is like a white out. Rage and violence can ensue when a reservoir of old, untapped feelings is triggered.

Once an episode like this is over, both parties are often so worn out and exhausted that they just want life to get back to normal. They don't often take the time to deconstruct the episode and figure out what really happened. After spending so much time fighting, they feel that they simply need to get back to the business of life. The unaddressed feelings are never properly dealt with, and they eventually get retriggered down the road, and another episode occurs.

These episodes are often the result of unprocessed feelings from childhood or early life. They can also result from unprocessed feelings in adulthood, but usually the root is in early experiences that were painful or traumatic. In these early experiences, the child was emotionally stymied and unable to process what they were feeling. The result is an accumulation of stuck and buried feelings deep inside.

As these feelings accumulate, it becomes more and more difficult for a person to be comfortable in their own skin. Carrying a heavy load of unprocessed emotional material takes a toll and creates a chronic sense of discomfort and unease. Over time, more unprocessed feelings layer one on top of another, and thus the discomfort continues to grow and intensify.

Eventually, the discomfort will become unbearable, and you will have to do something in order to feel relief. You simply won't be able to stand being with yourself anymore. This is a setup for dissociating from yourself and acting out in some way. It may feel like all that matters is finding a way to disconnect from yourself and your feelings.

Acting out in order to dissociate from yourself can take many forms. Binge eating, taking drugs, drinking alcohol, working compulsively, being sexually compulsive, addicting yourself to love and relationships, addicting yourself to electronics, gambling, and compulsive spending are just some of the most popular ways to dissociate.

These addictions and compulsive behaviors allow you to be physically present in a situation but not be there mentally or emotionally. Because you are mentally obsessed and physically preoccupied with your compulsions to act out, this keeps you from truly being with yourself or others. Through addictions and compulsions, you avoid feeling your feelings and check out of your life while appearing like you're there.

For many, dissociation starts out as a survival skill and is used to cope with emotional pain resulting from an unmanageable life situation. Because it is too uncomfortable to face everything at once, we find ways to check out for a while and get some relief. But eventually, dissociation can take on a life of its own and can even fuel lifelong addictions. It can become life-threatening and crippling to the soul. Whenever we dissociate, we are not dealing with what we are feeling and are using a substitute behavior or chemical to allow us to anesthetize ourselves.

There are two primary types of addictions: chemical addictions and process addictions. With chemical addictions, we ingest an external substance to change our emotional state and numb ourselves. It often requires more and more of the substance to get the same numbing effect over time. As we develop a tolerance to our numbing agents, we can get to the point where they don't work at all. That is when things get tough, and many people hit rock bottom. They end up between a rock and a hard place, because nothing works any more.

With process addictions, we engage in a

behavior that also gives us a chemical hit, but this time the chemical comes from our own body. Our own hormones and endo-chemicals can be very pleasurable and addictive. For instance, when we exercise, we get a nice hit of endorphins, one of nature's feel-good biochemicals. The same goes for sex; it gives us a nice dose of calming and comforting endo-chemicals. Eating food is another convenient way that we can seek self-soothing and pleasure on a regular basis.

To the addictive mind, if a little is good, more is better, and there is never enough of anything. We grab more and more of everything that soothes us and gives us pleasure, often crossing the invisible line into the zone of never-never land. When this happens, buried feelings can sit for years, hidden under increasing layers of feelings, behaviors, chemicals, and suffocating forces that keep them from ever reaching the surface and being processed.

Anger can be one of the most caustic internalized feelings. Suppressed anger can fester in the heart and mind for years. In and of itself, anger is a healthy emotion. It is a signal that there is something wrong or something that needs to change. It is a powerful energy source and a call to action. However, when anger is stored and suppressed, it can turn into a cascade of traumatizing behaviors inflicted upon oneself and other people. Many people are taught to deny their anger, but it never really goes away. If it is stuck inside, it can turn into resentment and can eventually morph into rage or violence. It is healthy to recognize your anger as promptly as you can and do something to address it before it turns into a monster.

If you have experienced emotional trauma, you may have a great deal of suppressed anger about your experiences and the way that you were treated. If you have not been able to express your anger, it is important to recognize it and deal with it head on.

Underneath anger and anxiety, you will often find find hurt. Hurt is the unaddressed and unprocessed pain that we feel when we experience emotional trauma. Hurt turns into stored grief, and stored trauma and grief can easily lay the foundation for other mental health problems like anxiety, depression, and various kinds of addictions.

There are many emotional and physical symptoms of stored trauma. They often present as symptoms of stress. As trauma accumulates over time and is unrecognized and unprocessed, the stress threshold can get lower and lower. You will find that you have more intense reactions to less stress and that it takes very little to put you over the edge.

The body and mind can only hold so much stress at one time until it begins to suffer. You may be able to identify certain parts of the body that are trying to get your attention after you have been traumatized or when old wounds have been reactivated. People often report feeling symptoms in their stomach, back, head, heart, and central nervous system. If a current stressor is removed and the symptoms go away, you know that this may be a physical reaction to stored trauma in the body.

Give yourself permission to feel whatever you feel whenever you feel it. There is tremendous power in simply allowing our feelings to surface and to be whatever they are. We often get so caught up in how we think we should be feeling at a certain time or situation that we lose sight of what's really going on within us. We can get trapped in posturing and wearing a mask for the world, because we want other people's approval, and we feel like our feelings are wrong. We allow other people to dictate to us how we should be feeling rather than truly being ourselves.

Until we feel our feelings, we remain blocked from experiencing much of the true joy of life. Trapped and internalized feelings are a barrier that prevents others from getting in. Trauma can also act as a barrier to our true self, which wants come out and be expressed. When we are blocked by stored trauma, we limit our capacity to live fully and to experience the full range of human emotions, including joy, wonder, and awe. Feeling all our feelings allows us to be truly alive. We can't choose to have just one category of feelings. We need to feel all of them. We must experience pain in order to also experience joy.

3

IDENTIFY BEHAVIOR PATTERNS

Many of our maladaptive behavior patterns are directed not only towards others but also towards ourselves. Whatever we do to others, we tend to do even more strongly to ourselves. For example, if you are critical of other people, you are most likely even more critical of yourself. Being critical of others can be an unhealthy way of trying to lift yourself up as a response to your own low self-esteem. It usually alienates people and makes them keep their distance from you. If you criticize people in the name of helping them, examine your motives. If you really want to help them, try to think of more constructive ways to do that. People are more likely to listen to what you have to say if it is said with kindness and love.

Become aware of when hypercritical messages pop up seemingly out of nowhere in your mind. Remember that we choose our thoughts; they do not simply happen to us. We tend to believe that we are passive recipients of our thoughts and that they have a life of their own. The truth is that we choose our thoughts. So, if we have hypercritical thoughts in our minds, we are either consciously or unconsciously choosing to have them.

Ruminating on the fear of not being good enough and being judgmental towards oneself and others are choices we make.

Our hypercritical thoughts are the result of a maladaptive mental behavior pattern that we can control. We are not born this way; rather, we learned these behaviors because of what was happening around us. If we were surrounded by family dysfunction or unhealthy people growing up, we may have unconsciously learned to become one of them ourselves.

Self-criticism is even more insidious and difficult to identify than thinking critically of others. You might have a constant inner dialogue running through your mind throughout the day that tells you you're not good enough, you're not measuring up, you're not as good as other people, or what you are doing is wrong. This constant barrage of negativity can leave you feeling insecure and unworthy.

When you have a critical or negative voice in your head, ask yourself, "Who is talking right now?" or "Whose voice is this?" The next time you catch yourself criticizing yourself, stop in your tracks and replace your inner dialogue with more positive thoughts about yourself. You can even extend this to other people in your life. Every time you have an urge to think or speak something negative about someone, say something positive instead. There is nothing as powerful as trying to lift other people up. When you consciously make an effort to build up the people in your life, your self-worth and relationships will improve. Doing this will lift you up even more than it uplifts otheres.

A close cousin of self-criticism is shaming. Do you shame yourself or others? Ask yourself if you look for the worst in every encounter and then try to make it someone else's fault. If something does not go well, do you find a way to make it someone else's responsibility? Remember that everything that goes wrong and every negative emotion that you feel are not necessarily someone's fault. If you tend to shame yourself mercilessly, remember that you are just a human being.

Perhaps you have a good reason for your negative feelings. But rather than shaming yourself for what is, accept your emotions and try to build something constructive with them. No one thrives under a wet blanket of continuous self-shaming. If someone shamed you early in your life, you may tend shame yourself now. Recognize this behavior pattern and replace the shaming with affirming. Affirm yourself and others. This is one of the ways that self-worth grows, and it help others do the same.

Hypervigilance is another behavior pattern that results from trauma. With hypervigilance, we are hyper-aware of our surroundings, always scanning the environment and encounters with other people for the possibility of danger. The default feeling of not feeling safe causes us to be on the defensive even when it is not necessary.

With hypervigilance, it is hard to let your guard down and be vulnerable, which makes it a challenge to participate in intimate relationships and allow intimacy to grow. Hypervigilance can be very exhausting and draining and can cause you to sabotage yourself by leaving relationships before they have a chance to get off the ground. It often evolves as an adaptive survival skill in an unsafe environment but becomes a liability when it is no longer useful or necessary. When it is not needed, it can get in the way of the natural evolution and progression of your life and relationships.

Self-abandonment is another major issue for people struggling with self-esteem and worthiness. One way that this occurs is through codependency. Over-focusing on others is a form of self-abandonment and can cause you to neglect your own well-being and self-care. If pleasing someone else is more important than your own well-being, you may be unknowingly abandoning yourself. If you put another person before yourself to your own detriment, you are abandoning yourself.

When other people have abandoned you in your life, especially when you were a child, abandonment can become normalized. It becomes what you are used to experiencing from others and then you do it to yourself too. You may unconsciously expect others to abandon you, and thus you set yourself up to abandon yourself. You may put others first as a desperate measure to hold on to them at any cost and as a mechanism to control your relationships and keep others in your life, even though it is at your own expense.

Another manifestation of childhood abandonment is the tendency to get addicted to unavailable people. This can occur as the result of a parent who left you or was for some other reason emotionally or physically unavailable. Perhaps you see a pattern in your life of being highly attracted to people who are hard to get, those who are just out of reach, or those who you know are not right for you.

This happens a lot to people who had narcissistic or unavailable parents who might have been there physically but were otherwise preoccupied with themselves. They may have hooked you into serving them all the time and focusing on their needs, while yours were not considered. Breaking the addiction to the unavailable is very hard to do, because you develop automatic radar for unavailable people, and they feel like home. The reason they feel like home is because they embody similar characteristics to the unavailable members of your family of origin.

You might be unconsciously drawn to people who embody both the negative and positive characteristics of your early primary caretakers, but people tend to gravitate more to those who embody the negative characteristics. Thus, it can be very easy to unknowingly choose partners who resemble people who hurt you in early life. We are programmed to gravitate towards the familiar, even if the familiar is painful. If you meet someone who happens to be kind, sweet, and totally available to you, you might get bored. They simply don't feel right or hold your interest. You could end up in a never-ending and extremely painful cycle of being addicted to the unavailable, being abandoned, and being re-traumatized again and again.

The way to break this cycle is to make your unconscious patterns conscious and make different choices for yourself, even if they feel uncomfortable at first. Two people who have just met often don't have the same level of interest in each other. Usually, one person has more interest than the other. If you tend to be attracted to the unavailable, you are much better off if the other person is the one who has more interest in you than you have in them.

Decide that you don't want to be the one pining away for an unavailable potential partner. You can learn to choose healthy people who truly want you. You must work to do that if you want to break your pattern of being addicted to the unavailable. Learn to love those who love you first. Find someone who is relatively healthy and learn to love them. Remember that love is a decision, not a feeling.

If you have a significant history of emotional trauma, and you find yourself suddenly madly in love with someone, there is a high likelihood that this person is not a healthy choice for you. The odds are that you're being irresistibly drawn to someone who reminds you of someone you loved who wasn't available to you from your early life. You may chase this new, unavailable person in an effort to repair your old emotional wounds. But if you want to change your life, you must break your old patterns. You can learn to love healthy people who will love you back. You can learn to love someone who adds value to your life instead of pain and suffering. Break your old patterns, and your life will take on a whole new dimension.

The fear of rejection is something that plagues many people who have experienced emotional trauma resulting from abandonment by people they loved. When you have a fear of rejection, you may often stop yourself from ever getting out of the gate, because you are afraid of getting hurt. This can cause you to sabotage your relationships very early on, because of your overwhelming fears of intimacy, of potential abandonment, and of the resulting familiar emotional trauma of rejection. If the fear of rejection makes you not want to engage in relationships with other people, it is a handicap and must be addressed.

Experiencing rejection is extremely painful, but rejection will not kill you. Sometimes, rejection is a form of protection. There are times when people reject us not because there is something wrong with us but because they are not supposed to be in our lives. It is really in our best interest for them to leave. You can always trust the universe to take care of you. Have faith that when someone rejects you, it is probably for the best. You don't want to be involved with someone who is not a good fit for you, and if they reject you, it's highly possible that your relationship with them was not meant to last.

Maybe rejection will teach you something you needed to learn. Some relationships last for a moment, others for a season, and others for a lifetime. Our lifelong relationships are few and far between, but even the shorter ones teach us valuable lessons. We can take the good from them without being trapped in our feelings of rejection. We can trust that when someone leaves our life, there is a good reason for it, and it is for the best. Take whatever positives you can from having known them, try to release your resentments and grudges, and move forward in freedom.

Most dysfunctional families have members who play various roles: hero, lost child, mascot, peacemaker, or scapegoat. When it comes to abuse, the scapegoat is the one that receives and contains the negative feelings for the other family members. If you feel like people are always taking things out on you, you may be a scapegoat. It is not uncommon for the person who is the scapegoat to act out the pain of the family until they can't take it anymore. It is up to you to stop being a scapegoat and to stop letting people take things out on you. You are not meant to be the receptacle for other people's baggage. If you allow them to dump their baggage on to you, they will never take responsibility for it. You will keep accumulating their garbage, and you will pay a higher and higher price. It is up to you to say no and put a stop to it and let them deal with their own stuff. You deal with yours and let them deal with theirs.

False loyalty is another behavior pattern occurring in people who have experienced abuse. In many cases, the abuse began early in life and came from a parent or sibling. In these situations, the abusive people were your family and were also all that you had. Your very survival depended upon them. Since you looked to them for everything in life, you would never have considered betraying them or leaving them. You were dependent upon people who traumatized you, and you had to remain loyal, despite the abuse, in order to survive. This creates an unhealthy behavior pattern of false loyalty.

Emotional trauma sets you up to repeat this pattern with other people in your life as an adult. You might find that you continue to be loyal to people who hurt and abuse you. Even though they are traumatizing you, you can't leave them. The pull is so strong, and the connection feels so familiar, that you cannot leave them because it feels like you would be cutting off part of yourself. So, you stay connected to those who continue to hurt you and maintain a sense of loyalty to them, even though you have been repeatedly hurt and betrayed.

Breaking this pattern of false loyalty requires you to put yourself first. You have to decide that you are more important than others and that your well-being has to come first. If you don't look out for yourself, who will? Only you can do it. Other people may not like it, but if you begin to do it and keep it up, they will get used to the new you. And if they don't, that means they are not supposed to be in your life anymore, and that is okay. There are times in life when we must take stock of what we have brought into our world and declutter our lives from the things that no longer serve us.

When you decide to let go of unhealthy relationships, you will feel pain and grief, but that hurt will replaced by self-esteem, self-worth, and many new people and opportunities that will fill the void and enrich your life in countless ways. Once this happens, you will wonder why you waited so long to take the trash out. You will also find out that letting go of unhealthy attachments will not kill you. Although you may grieve, the grief will end. You will not mourn your losses forever, but rather, your life will be renewed and enriched in wonderful and positive ways by things you never could have imagined would come into your life. These will be things that you didn't even know you were missing until you get them. Every time that we let go of something that we need to release, we are practicing an act of faith. We are trusting that that empty space will be filled by something much better. This never fails to happen. You can count on it.

If you are holding on to someone or something that you know is not working, and you can't let it go because you're too afraid, just start by backing off a little bit. As you keep backing off, you will see that you are being taken care of and then your life is going to fill up with much better things. You have to face the fear of the grief and loss, let go of what doesn't belong in your life, and trust the universe to take good care of you.

As you go through this imperfect process of healing, you are bound to take steps both forwards and backwards. If you happen to take a step backwards, try not to shame yourself. You may tend to be hard on yourself and shame yourself at the drop of a hat, especially if you were shamed by others in the past. Recognize your self-shaming behaviors by your inner dialogue and the things that you tell yourself.

If you put yourself down, criticize yourself,

beat yourself up, and never give yourself a break, you probably have a long-standing pattern of shaming yourself. Whenever you catch yourself doing this, stop yourself in your tracks and tell yourself something positive about yourself. Remind yourself of how far you have come and all the good things that you are doing to heal. Affirm yourself, empower yourself, and encourage yourself. Even if no one else is doing it for you, you can still do it for yourself.

From time to time, an old trauma bubble may resurface and grab your attention. You might find yourself in intense emotional pain, and this can be frightening. If you find yourself recreating traumatic situations for yourself, you may be doing this as an unconscious lesson to yourself on how to get through it successfully once and for all.

Whenever old feelings come up, it is an opportunity for you to process them and get to a deeper level of healing. Give yourself permission to express what you feel as you go along in your journey. The only person who can shut you down is you. It is important to keep the channels open, and keep the process going. You will know when you have closed a chapter because it no longer grabs your attention. You will find that it simply is not an issue anymore, and you will experience a feeling of peace, tranquility, and neutrality that you didn't think you would ever have.

As the layers slowly peel off, you will continue to access deeper and deeper levels of healing. This can go on for a long time, and at times it may feel like it's never going to end. While some issues never completely go away, most heal to the point where they don't control you or cause major difficulties in your life anymore. They might end up as small voices that crop up from time to time rather than powerful forces that wreak havoc on your life. Seek progress, not perfection. As you do your own work, you will continue to make progress as time goes on. The more progress you make, the more important it is to remember how far you've come. At a certain point you will barely recognize yourself, because you will be a transformed human being.

4

IDENTIFY BELIEFS

HOW TO HEAL EMOTIONAL TRAUMA

Emotional trauma can cause disproportionate feelings of self-doubt and fear. Fear can be a paralyzing and pervasive feeling that controls your life and choices. Fear is the root of much pain and suffering. Rooting out your fears well dispel a great deal of negativity in your life. Your fears can be dealt with one by one as you become more and more aware of what they are. They will not come up all at once. If a particular fear continues to present itself, you will be given repeated opportunities to conquer the issue and master the lesson it is giving you. Take the teaching as soon as you can so that you do not have to waste too many years learning the same thing over and over again.

Remember that fear is just a feeling. There are healthy fears, and there are also unhealthy and unrealistic fears that will never come to pass. Being afraid of being hit by a moving truck if you walk out into the middle of the highway is a realistic and healthy fear. We need some fear to protect us. However, unhealthy fears can cripple us and cause us to live partial lives. It can be very challenging to identify our fears when they are wrapped in layers of defenses and dysfunctional behavior patterns. Take the time to unpack your fears thoroughly. Most fears can be conquered if you face them head on.

If you do the thing that you fear, the death of that fear is certain. Many of our fears have been created by our own minds or learned from others who influenced us, only to grow larger over time because we hide from them and give them power. The way to take power away from your fears is to confront them and assess what is real and what is not. When it comes to the imagined fears that only exist and grow in our minds, we have the power to renew our minds, root out these fears, and cast them aside.

It is helpful to talk to another person about your fears to get a balanced perspective. It can be very difficult to correct what is wrong with you, namely faulty thinking, with only your own faulty thinking. Talk to someone you trust about what you are fearful of, and sort it out. You will be guided on what to do and when to do it. Decide that you no longer want your life to be controlled by fear, and you will be well on your way. So many of our problems boil down to unaddressed and unresolved fears. When we bring these out into the light of day, they frequently disappear. The light always overcomes the dark.

One of the primary issues resulting from stored emotional trauma is the tendency to view the world antagonistically. Because you have been hurt, often by the only people who took care of you and who you trusted, the world doesn't feel like a safe place. You can feel that everyone is going to hurt you and that if you let them in and get close to them, they will cause you pain. You may adopt a defensive posture in life to protect yourself.

Although there is some pain and conflict involved in all intimate relationships, most people are not out to get you. Viewing the world antagonistically puts you in a passive and paranoid position where you will find yourself in adversarial situations when you don't need to be. You will perceive encounters as conflicts rather than as opportunities to join and work together. When you approach situations as though they are conflicts, you are set up for competitive win-lose dynamics which are not conducive to harmony, cooperation, and love. If someone always wins, someone else always loses, and no one is safe. Going through life in this fashion can leave you devoid of loving and trusting relationships. And those types of relationships are the number one factor associated with happiness and life satisfaction.

Many people who have lived with the effects of emotional trauma create self-imposed psychological prisons. This means that they impose a rigid set of beliefs upon themselves which they use to try to feel safe and survive.

These fixed beliefs can be helpful at first, but they can also become quite limiting if they don't allow you to expand, grow, and thrive.

For example, if you tell yourself that it is not safe to talk to people that you don't know, it becomes very difficult to meet anyone new. Being afraid of people is a common effect of emotional trauma, because most emotional trauma is caused by people. It is very easy to fear people rather than to want to connect with them and enjoy them. It can feel like a great burden to have to deal with people. In a healthy mindset, people are what make us feel alive and help us thrive. In healthy relationships, we seek connection with people to give and receive love and support.

In toxic relationships, people are feared and often experienced as a source of pain. If that is how you feel, then you may avoid people. You may feel that it is easier to be alone and that it is too much trouble to deal with others. This can lead to isolation. Isolation is one of the most dangerous things for human beings. It is in isolation that we go crazy, shrivel up, and wither away. When we only have our own minds and our own voice to listen to, things can get very strange.

Remember that you cannot fix your thinking with your own thinking if your thinking is unhealthy. That is why we need others to share ideas, to talk about what is really going on, and to get reality checks about life. An important part of mental health is having healthy relationships and connections with others. It is through connection with other human beings that we truly heal and grow.

Another example of a self-limiting belief is when we tell ourselves that things will never change. We may convince ourselves that we are the way we are, that's the way it is, it's always going to be this way, and we can't get better. This is a lie. Whether we tell ourselves this lie about ourselves or others, it is a self-limiting idea that needs to be shed. If we convince ourselves that we can never change, we are giving up. It means we tell ourselves that we have done all the growing that we will ever do, and that we're done. This is an excuse for laziness, apathy, or the fear of doing the internal work that we need.

The fact is, anyone can change when they decide they want to. Change begins first on the inside, when we alter what we believe. The first step to change is to believe that change is possible. This is the jumping point from which everything else happens. Once we truly believe that change is possible, we start to take new action in our lives. We will start to do things differently, and we see results.

The same actions tend to produce the same results, but new actions will produce new results. Once you see meaningful change, it will continue to build cumulatively, one change upon another, progressing incrementally over a long period, and eventually leading to a completely transformed person and renewed life.

Self-limiting beliefs can also take the form of thinking that you don't belong or that you are an outsider. This is a common feeling among people who have experienced emotional trauma. No matter where they go, what they do, or how much they accomplish, they never feel quite good enough, and they always feel like they don't belong. Even though others may see them as the "in-crowd," they always feel like the "out-crowd."

This can begin with your family of origin if you felt like you didn't belong in it. If you felt disconnected and unable to relate to your family members, you are likely to carry that feeling forward in other areas of life. You may feel like an outsider no matter where you are. That precious sense of belonging can be ever-elusive. The fact is that many people feel this way, and it is almost a universal part of the human condition. A lot of the people who seem to have it all together feel exactly as you do. They too feel like outsiders.

This sense of feeling like you don't belong can be rooted in shame. Shame is a dark and stifling cloud that can follow you everywhere you go, making you feel like you just aren't good enough. While guilt tends to relate to a specific action, shame is more about who you are. Shame tells you that you are eternally defective and that you will never be good enough. It tells you that you are not as good as other people and are inherently incapable of becoming good enough, because there is just something about you that is defective or less than other people. The pervasiveness and destructiveness of this emotion is hard to overstate. We can carry this feeling around with us for years just like we're wearing a dirty, itchy sweater, and we may not even know that we have shame until it's gone.

Toxic shame is not the same thing as having healthy discernment and a good moral compass. We all need to be able to distinguish right from wrong, and we all make mistakes at times and miss the mark. Appropriate guilt when we misbehave is healthy, because it helps us to correct ourselves and do better next time. Toxic shame, on the other hand, is an enduring pervasive belief that we are bad people, and this faulty belief is not something that is ever going to help us do better in life. While you need to take responsibility for yourself and your shortcomings, you must always remember that you are a good person trying to do better, not a bad person doomed to always be bad.

Both abandonment and psychological abuse can create toxic shame. Abandonment creates shame because we feel like it was our fault that other people left our lives when we needed or wanted them there. We blame ourselves for their leaving, when in most cases their leaving had nothing to do with us at all. It was all about their agenda and their issues. But if you were abandoned, particularly as a child, it is difficult to know that and not blame yourself. This can leave you with a chronic sense of shame and fear of abandonment in your relationships in the future.

The unconscious fear of abandonment can stay with you throughout life and can be reactivated at times by both real and imagined situations. It can wreak havoc on your peace of mind, and it can also sabotage your relationships. When you repeatedly act irrationally out of fear and impose unrealistic expectations upon people, you may drive them away. You may fear abandonment so much that you begin to see your relationships through the lens of abandonment and think that people are abandoning you all the time, even when they are not. This can be very exhausting for your loved ones, who might feel like they can never do it right and thus become tired of you.

In this way, shame and fear of abandonment can put great stress and strain on intimate relationships and can cause you to sabotage yourself. Sometimes the fear of abandonment is so great that you can end up bringing abandonment upon yourself to put an end to the fear. When this happens, you no longer have to feel afraid. The abandonment has already taken place. However, that is likely to leave you in a deep emotional pit from which it takes great effort to dig out. It is better to do the emotional work and get to the root of your fear of abandonment so that it does not drive you or sabotage your relationships. What we fear the most is what we often end up bringing about in our lives. For this reason, it is very important to believe that we can recover and heal from our emotional trauma.

One manifestation of the fear of abandonment is the tendency to chase unavailable people. If you had a parent or primary relationship in early life who either abandoned you or was unavailable to you due to dysfunction or addiction, you may have a pattern of going after what you can't have. When you seek intimacy from someone who is unavailable or who gives you crumbs intermittently, it is easy to get caught up in an addictive cycle of trying to get bread from the hardware store. If you never get anything from someone, is easier to get the message that there is nothing there for you and to move on. However, if you receive occasional reinforcement, that can keep you in an endless cycle of going back and chasing for more and trying to repair the deficits of your early life.

If your needs were not met from the people who were supposed to love you when you were young, you may unconsciously choose people who are unavailable when you are an adult and chase them relentlessly to try to get what you missed out on earlier in life. Chasing behavior is a reaction to our childhood fear of abandonment. You are most likely to keep doing it until the frustration outweighs any payoff. Even then, it takes time to let go and walk away.

Psychological abuse can create shame when we blame ourselves for the abuse. We tell ourselves that we were abused because we deserved it and that it is our fault. This leads to a spiral of negativity where we feel badly about ourselves because of what happened, and that creates more shame and more bad feelings about who we are. We may be afraid to talk about it, because we fear that people will judge and blame us as some of our dysfunctional family members might have done. No one ever should feel shame for having experienced emotional trauma. It does not happen because you have done something to deserve it. It happens because someone else did not deal with their own issues, and they took them out on you.

While it is relatively hard to completely shed the fear of abandonment, shame is different. The good news about shame is that it can go away. When shame lifts, you literally feel like a new person. You look different, you carry yourself differently, you speak differently, your posture is different, and your energy vibrations are different. People notice, and they start reacting differently to you. They can see that you feel good about yourself and that you respect yourself. If you respect yourself, they will follow your lead. Others will begin to treat you better than you have ever been treated before. You will feel their respect, admiration, and love.

This is all because you are giving it to yourself first. Whatever you give to yourself is what you give to others and also what others give back to you. You start treating other people differently when your shame lessens. You will become a more open and honest person, able to give and receive love freely. You will not be afraid of other people's judgments and disapproval because you approve of yourself. It really does begin with you.

Feeling responsible for what other people do is also a manifestation of emotional trauma. Being conditioned to take responsibility for other people's choices is a hallmark of dysfunctional families, where the entire family is one ego mass. There is often a high level of codependency, and there is little psychological differentiation between family members. In a codependent family system, you don't know where you end and where others begin. If something happens to one person, it feels like it is happening to everyone. There are not a lot of boundaries around feelings, so if one person is feeling something, everyone tends to have the same feeling.

This can lead to a sense of inappropriate responsibility about what others are feeling and doing. When there is no separation and individuation, it is hard to remember that you are you, and they are them, and different people can do things very differently. When you feel responsible for what other people do, you are in a passive and dependent position. Your emotional state is determined by someone else, not by you. This can create a great deal of depression, control issues, hostility, anxiety, and anger.

The fact is, you are only responsible for

yourself. You are only responsible for what you think and for what you say and do. Only your choices fall under your control, so you can allow other people to make their own choices and be whoever they want to be. Give them the dignity of making their own choices, of being the author of their own story, and of being the architect of their own lives.

If someone close to you gets into a difficulty, you don't need to feel ashamed about it. You didn't do it; they did. While you can have empathy and compassion for them and even try to help them, you don't have to carry their burden or feel their feelings for them. Let them have their own feelings. Remember, they need to feel the full range of their feelings to learn their own lessons, make changes, and grow. Stay in your own lane, focus on your own life, and let them do the same.

Seeking negative excitement is another way that we can sabotage ourselves. Some people seek out negative excitement because it feels familiar to them, and it makes them feel alive. If you grew up in a chaotic, traumatic, or abusive environment, there were probably a lot of negative events that occurred. Is important to recognize that these negative events were not healthy or exciting. They were drama and trauma. If you have gotten used to drama, you might feel empty or lifeless without it. There are plenty of other ways to add richness and vibrancy to your life that have nothing to do with negative excitement and chaos.

Negative excitement also has a way of distracting you from yourself and can be a way of avoiding your own life. Ask yourself whether you might unconsciously be drawn to chaos, and if you are, shift that energy into constructive and positive pursuits in your life. Letting other people's chaos drain you and steal away your time is a way of wasting your own life. Use your time, energy, and other resources to enrich your life and those of the people you love in a healthy, constructive, and positive way.

One of the most important things to realize about emotional trauma is that you did not deserve it. Very often, the ones who abuse you tell you that they're doing what they're doing because of something you have done and that the abuse is your fault. They can be cunning and manipulative in convincing you either that you deserve it or that the abuse is not really happening. This gaslighting behavior is extremely damaging, because it makes an individual question their own sanity and perceptions. When you see something right in front of your face and someone is telling you that is not happening, it is very disorienting and confusing.

Psychological abuse will keep you off balance and cause you to second guess yourself. It is important to remember that not only do you not deserve it, but whatever you thought was happening was happening. You are not crazy, and you have not made anything up. People who tell you that you're exaggerating, that you're too sensitive, that it's all in your head, and that you're crazy are abusing you even more by saying these things to you.

Whatever you feel is valid. Trust yourself and your perceptions. Trust what you know more than what others say. You are the one experiencing it, and it is up to you stand with yourself and honor your truth. Once you recognize your self-limiting beliefs, you can change them. Once you realize that your thinking is turning negative, put a stop to it. Don't follow a line of thought that is only going to lead you to suffering. You can choose your thoughts and beliefs, and you can unlearn whatever has been learned in. Keep your thinking positive, look for the good in every situation, and stay true to yourself.

5

STOP ACCEPTING ABUSE AND SELF-SABOTAGE

When you have been emotionally traumatized for a long time, stored trauma becomes a part of you. It can be difficult to recognize that you have been abused. Abuse becomes normalized and familiar, and you may start to expect most relationships to feel this way. At the unconscious level, you may even seek out people who continue to abuse you and not realize what you are doing. It is like you have an innate radar to find the one person in a crowd who will make you feel just like all the others did. The same issues are reincarnated in every relationship until they are resolved, and you will continue to be retraumatized until you finally break the cycle.

Breaking the cycle requires you to first become conscious of your habit patterns and to understand what you have experienced earlier in your life. This is key to understanding the reasons why these patterns persist. As with many long-term issues, you need to hit bottom before you truly wake up and are ready and willing to change. Coming out of denial can be a painful process and one that can take a long time. As time goes on and as you continue to experience the same painful feelings, you will begin to ask yourself why this keeps happening to you. Each time, you will move closer to breaking the cycle as your tolerance for the pain decreases. The common denominator in these situations is you. While it may be convenient to keep blaming others, you are the one who is choosing the people who hurt you and accepting their abusive behavior.

One form of self-abuse is self-punishment or self-humiliation. When we have experienced a great deal of shaming or humiliation from people who have behaved abusively towards us, we find ways shame or humiliate ourselves. Although we know intellectually that it is a bad thing, we can get so used to the painful feelings that we don't feel right unless we experience them. We can get so used to humiliation that we seek it out, because we believe we deserve it and that it is the natural order of things.

We will continue to find new perpetrators who are happy to do to us what we've experienced from other people earlier in our lives. We are drawn to them like magnets, because they feel so familiar. When it feels like love at first sight, you have probably stumbled upon someone who is a replica of an original perpetrator who was abusive to you. Your radar has found a match for your neurosis. When this happens, run. Unless you want to spend years reliving the past, resist the pull of this irresistible magnet. It is most likely only going to cause you a lot of pain.

Repressed anger is one of the main culprits of the phenomenon of self-abuse. This occurs when anger is suppressed and layers upon itself over a long period. Eventually, repressed anger can become so controlling that it can cause you to harm both yourself and others.

Many people are taught that it is not acceptable to be angry. Women are particularly discouraged from openly expressing anger, while men are given more permission to have it. Some families discourage any expression of anger because of a family culture of emotional denial and repression. If you have grown up in a family culture that disavows anger, you most likely have repressed a great deal of it in your life.

We all feel anger, and it is a normal, healthy emotion. Anger is simply a signal that there is something wrong or something we need to change or attend to. Anger, fear, and anxiety all give us the drive and energy that we need to make changes and do things with our lives. If we don't allow ourselves to feel our anger, we set ourselves up to either explode or implode later on.

There tend to be two types of people. The first are those whose anger turns inward, which can lead to depression. The second type are those whose anger gets directed outward. These people can become hostile, alienating, or even violent towards others. Very often, an outwardly expressive angry person will bully the type of person who internalizes and holds on to their anger. The latter is the type of person who experiences emotional trauma for a long period without doing anything about it. The fear of the angry person in their life creates a depressive passivity which perpetuates the cycle.

Sometimes, a health crisis is required to usher in a new way of life for the person who has repressed their anger. This can take the form of depression, anxiety, heart problems, nervous system problems, sleep issues, and emotional illness or outbursts. Eventually, a person who is repressing his or her anger will hit some sort of a bottom. An individual may become conscious of his or her issues very slowly, but sometimes it can also happen suddenly.

When you come to the end of the road, you will simply have a feeling that you cannot take it anymore. You will wake up and have a new perspective on yourself and your life that is different from anything you will have ever experienced. You will be able to connect the dots and become more fully conscious not only of what drives you but also of the fact that you need to create change in your life. You will have a certainty about this like you have never had before. This is when your new life begins. Welcome to new territory.

At the point when you have an inner shift, and you decide that you are no longer going to tolerate abuse, you will feel like you have been let out of prison and are free for the first time. It is an extraordinary feeling to know that you can create massive change in your future and that no one has any power over you unless you give it to them. The simple fact is that you do not have to take abuse if you decide not to.

Self-abuse can also manifest as self-neglect. Many people who have experienced trauma were not only traumatized by parents or other people in their lives but also were neglected. Neglect is often subtle and difficult to identify, but if you think about your history, you may begin to realize that this was an issue for you. If your caregivers were unavailable, did not respond to you, did not ask or care about how you felt, or were dismissive towards you, you may have experienced neglect. People who have experienced neglect often grow up with a feeling that they just don't matter, and they continue to feel this way in their adult lives. They didn't feel valued as children, and they tend to carry that same feeling into adulthood.

If you continue to feel as though you just don't matter, despite evidence to the contrary, you probably experienced a great deal of neglect earlier in your life and did not know it. One of the problems with having been neglected is that we tend to learn to neglect ourselves as adults. We discount ourselves and our value and don't treat ourselves as though we matter, because no one else ever did. We abandon ourselves and disregard our own feelings, wants, and needs, because we are not even on our own radar screen. We often choose narcissistic friends and partners and tend to become overly focused on them, all the while neglecting ourselves. This is a form of self-abuse. When we don't matter enough to ourselves, we don't take care of ourselves, and we let other people walk all over us. They become the priority in our lives and our whole world revolves around them. Recognizing self-neglect is one of the critical first steps to building self-worth.

First, you must realize that you exist, and then you can realize that you matter. Once you know that you deserve to have a central place in your own life, you can evolve beyond your old patterns of self-neglect and self-abuse and start to value yourself. It is up to you to do this, and only you can do it. As you begin to pay attention to yourself, you will inevitably start noticing what needs to be done to take good care of yourself. This is the key building block to your new way of life and will result in a feeling of strength and value.

Once you feel a sense of inner strength and freedom, you will have turned the corner. You will begin to make choices that you have never made before. Setting healthy boundaries with others will become much easier, and you will consider your well-being in all your choices and encounters. While you were previously not a factor in your choices because they revolved around other people, you will become the most important person in your life. You will start to feel as though you have a newfound confidence and you have the courage to do whatever you need to do to take care of yourself. This does not have to be at the expense of others. You are standing up for yourself, not against others.

In order to stop accepting abuse, you may need to remove yourself from certain situations and people. As you start to make different choices, you will probably let go of some toxic and unhealthy people in your life. When people show you who they really are, believe them. This will be easier to do with some people than with others.

If toxic people are in your family, you may not be able to completely cut them out of your life. In these cases, you can simply minimize your contact with them and focus your energy on those you want to spend time with. Even minimizing contact will make a difference in your life. Remember that you are in control and they are not. With acquaintances and peripheral friends, it is much easier to set limits and boundaries and back away from those relationships. You can either do it slowly, or you can simply say goodbye. Do whatever works better for you. Remember that you don't have to keep anyone in your life who mistreats you or makes you feel badly about yourself.

Another form of self-abuse is taking on too much in your life. You can overburden yourself to no end with activities, and that can create a chronic sense of unmanageability and overload. If you find yourself constantly feeling like you never have enough time and always have too much to do, take stock of how you spend your time. Do an inventory of your daily and weekly obligations and use of time, and see if you have balance in your life. Look at your commitments, and ask yourself what is truly necessary and what may be optional. Let go of some activities if you are not handling the basics first.

Taking on too much can be rooted in a tendency towards over-responsibility. This means that you feel responsible for everything, even things that you shouldn't feel responsible for. You may be taking on other people's responsibilities and neglecting your own. Remember that your own life is your primary responsibility and that other people are responsible for their own lives too. Ask yourself, "What am I doing," "Who am I doing it for," and "Why am I doing it?" These three questions will give you a lot of valuable information about your use of time and your priorities.

Perfectionism is another issue to examine. On the surface, it can seem like a good thing, because you are trying to be excellent. However, when you take a deeper look at perfectionism, you will find it is a never-ending battle of not feeling good enough and can prevent you from being your authentic self. Perfectionism always asks the question, "Will I be good enough?" With perfectionism, there is no end. There is always more you can do; there is always a way to be better; and you can feel like you are never ever enough.

Perfectionism can evolve as the result of trying to please people who were very critical and difficult to please. If these people were emotionally abusive, you might have come to believe that if you were more perfect, they would give you the love that you wanted and stop treating you badly. If you think that you might be a perfectionist, you probably are. Although some people need higher standards, others need lower ones. You may experience more joy, peace, and serenity if you dare to be more ordinary. You will still end up far above average. Give yourself a break, stop being so hard on yourself, and let yourself be imperfect like the rest of the world. There is no perfect, and you cannot spend your whole life trying to reach a standard that doesn't exist.

People who had "perfect" childhoods often don't do as well in life. While they may look great on the outside, there is always more than meets the eye lurking on the inside. Even those who had stellar role models and family lives can be challenged as adults. They often don't have the same drive to advance themselves later in life because they have not experienced inner discomfort and pain. Pain and discomfort can be character-building and a great gift when it motivates us to seek positive growth and change.

Criticizing yourself without mercy is another self-sabotaging behavior. If you feel like everything is your fault and that you are always wrong, recognize that you are abusing yourself. You have let your inner critical voice take over and run the show. Once you recognize that the inner critic is in control, you can stop it and replace the inner critic with your own loving voice. You can start to tell yourself loving things about yourself and others and experience a profound shift in your attitude towards yourself and life. Even if you can't completely silence the internal critical voice, you can integrate it. Once the volume is turned down, and it is softened, it will lose its grip on you.

Using humor to laugh off your trauma is another way to discount yourself. In doing so, you dismiss abusive behavior and devalue yourself. If you laugh off other people's abusive behavior towards you, you are passively condoning it. You're sending a message that it really doesn't matter, that you don't really matter, and that your feelings don't really matter. Using humor to laugh off abuse is usually done as part of a people-pleasing scenario. You may be trying to make other people feel comfortable, perhaps joining in on their laughter, and not dealing directly with what happened. It can be an excuse for not facing the situation honestly, being true to yourself, and taking care of yourself. It is a cop out.

You don't need to work hard at making abusive people feel comfortable. That is part of the dysfunctional hold that they have on you in the first place. So why spend your energy taking care of their feelings when they are not taking care of yours? Part of the abusive cycle is when others get you to focus too much on them and not enough on yourself. When you bring your focus back on yourself, you will realize that what they are doing to you is not cute or funny. It is mean and nasty, and you don't have to take it. You can stand up for yourself and put a stop to it. You are the one allowing it to continue, and laughing it off is another way of prolonging the pain.

You can become so used to abuse that things just don't feel right when you're not being abused. If you don't have anyone else doing it to you, you will do it to yourself. Here are some of the many ways that you can abuse yourself: binge eating, overworking, compulsive activity, overspending, electronics addiction, sexual addiction, compulsive rebellion, gambling, the unconscious seeking out of addictive or abusive relationships, drugs, alcohol, and the compulsive seeking out of endo-chemicals like adrenaline, cortisol, and dopamine.

Let's look at the example of binge eating. With compulsive food behaviors, people often report that they feel like they are abusing themselves with food. They are not eating because they are hungry, but rather, they are eating to try to anaesthetize the painful feelings that are inside of them. Having a binge with food can leave you feeling so sick that it's equivalent to beating yourself up. This is a form of self-abuse. When you eat to the point of injuring yourself, either quickly or slowly, you are using food to punish yourself and to harm yourself. This is done because the pain of the food abuse is easier to tolerate than the pain of life. It is only by addressing the unprocessed feelings inside of you that you can stop the compulsive behavior and become free. It is not so much about what you are eating as it is about what is eating you. When you dig deep, get to the root of the problem, and address the true inner disturbance, then the external self-destructive behaviors will diminish.

The same dynamic applies to all the other addictions and self-abusive behaviors. As long as you are abusing yourself in any way, all you are dealing with is the fallout of the pain from your self-abuse. You are avoiding dealing with what's really going on inside of you. You can spend years switching self-abusive behaviors and never really get to the core issues that are going on inside. Once you realize that you are abusing yourself because a new form of pain is easier to tolerate then your baseline pain, you can decide that you are going to stop acting out and allow yourself to deal with the real issues rather than the cheap substitutes.

Becoming aware of self-abuse is essential for the development of self-worth. Most people don't know that they are abusing themselves or using other people to do it for them. It takes a lot of deconstructing and soul searching to really get honest and recognize what you are doing. Once you are aware of your self-sabotage and abuse, you are more than halfway there. It is very difficult to continue to harm yourself when you know what you are doing. When you realize that you are choosing the harm and choosing the pain and that you have the option to make different choices, it becomes much easier to connect the dots, let go, and move on.

Many of the self-abusive scenarios that we create are done in isolation. Some of them are done in the privacy of our homes, and we never talk about what we're doing. We use our self-abusive behaviors as secret coping mechanisms to get us through the pain of each day. We feel like it is okay if no one knows and we look okay on the outside. Isolation cuts us off from getting help and healing, and it fuels the unhealthy behaviors even more.

Once we get out of isolation and start honestly talking about what we are really doing, we have already decided that we going to change. When we release ourselves from our self-imposed prisons and begin to share with someone we trust what we are doing, thinking, and feeling, change will naturally occur.

Although it may feel scary in the beginning, because we don't easily trust people, it will become easier the more we do it. The more we share about our self-sabotaging behaviors with our support system, the more power we take away from those behaviors. Maladaptive coping mechanisms will be replaced by new and more healthy coping strategies that will leave us feeling loved, supported, and fulfilled. As we get out of isolation, deprogram, and reprogram the inner critical voices, we will begin to realize that we are not as sick or unique as we thought we were. We will also realize that we are good enough, and that there are many people out there in the world who love us and whom we can also trust and love.

6

LETTING GO OF THE VICTIM MENTALITY

Many people adopt a victim mentality without realizing it. What this can mean is that you see yourself and your life situations through the lens of a victim. You are the one who is slighted, cheated, hurt, and abused by others. You see it as all their fault and as a victim, have difficulty taking responsibility for your own part in the situation. You may ask, "What do you mean, MY part? I'm the one who was hurt and abused..." Your part might be that you chose them, stayed with them, and ignored the red flags that you saw in the beginning.

Many people do this by rationalizing the things that they see because they want their fantasy version of the other person and don't want to face reality. Or they sell out, because they get something else that they want from the relationship as part of the package. Money is one example of this. If you settle for less than what you actually need in a relationship, you will experience chronic dissatisfaction.

Money can never make up for lack of love. Staying with someone who is abusing you because they have a lot of money is very expensive. You are paying the high price of your dignity to have access to financial security. Ask yourself if it is worth it. For some, it may be worth it for a while but not forever. Although not being able to meet your own needs financially is difficult, you always have the option to work and earn money. It is very difficult to go through life without feeling valued and loved. Many people in this situation eventually come to a point where they realize that the money just isn't worth it.

Our internalized, critical voices can tell us that we are not good enough, and that is the same voice that also blames others. Blame is an integral part of the victim mentality. In order to be a victim, you have to be a victim of something or somebody. There is always a reason outside of yourself that you use to explain why you are where you are. And in most cases, the thing that we are victimized by is something that we feel we have absolutely no control over. That means there's nothing we can do about it except feel like a victim. If you find yourself blaming others a lot, criticizing them in your mind, and wishing that they would change, you are setting yourself up to feel like a victim.

This critical inner voice might tell you that you're not good enough, but it also tells you that others are not good enough. If you repeatedly find yourself in situations where you feel wronged by others, stop and ask yourself how you are participating in this dynamic. Are you inviting poor treatment or accepting bad behavior that you don't have to tolerate?

It is up to you to set the limits that you need and to teach people how to treat you. This is best done early in a relationship, otherwise negative patterns tend to set in. If there has been a longstanding pattern of abusive behavior in your relationship, you can still change your part of the relationship dynamic. It is never too late to change yourself and set new boundaries with others. You can also improve your communication skills and become clearer about who you are and what you need.

You might be afraid to shake things up out of fear that people will abandon you. However, if you can't be the best version of yourself with someone, why be with them? If you choose to be around negative people who drag you down and shame you, you will just sink along with them. It is up to you to put a stop to it.

In order to do this, you first have to change your thinking. This means that you need to start believing that you deserve more. It also means that you must believe you have the strength to make the changes you need and accept the outcome. If someone leaves your life, and they were not supposed to be in it in the first place, you are doing yourself a favor by accepting it without a fight. This will make room for better things to come into your life and for you to live more authentically and become happier and more fulfilled.

Another way that you can take responsibility is to ask yourself why you keep coming back for more. Even if you did not initially see that there was abusive behavior ahead, once you know, it is your responsibility to take care of yourself and leave if you need to. If you are continuing to go back for more when you should be walking away, you are choosing to be a victim. Some people get a payoff from being a victim because they don't want to take full responsibility for themselves. They don't want to grow up and be adults. It is easier to remain a dependent child who is being abused than it is to grow up and take control of your life. Being a victim and living in constant reaction to others allows them to drain and distract you from your own life. You end up living in reaction to them as opposed to focusing on and building your own life.

Being a victim also puts you in a dependent state. Your well-being and emotions are dependent on the person who is victimizing you. This can lead to an incredible reservoir of resentment. If you continue to feel victimized, this resentment can continue to build and build until it turns into hate. Many people-pleasers are also conditioned to never ever hate anyone and to always try to be nice. Being nice can be hazardous to your health and can leave you feeling victimized and resentful.

There are times when it is much better to get angry than to feel self-pity and fall into the victim mindset. There is a difference between healthy hate and unhealthy hate. Unhealthy hate is a corrosive emotion that eat up your insides. It makes you feel physically ill and is very toxic. On the other hand, healthy hate can be very useful if it is part of an emotional bottom that causes you to set boundaries and start making changes in your life. Sometimes we just need to get angry enough to not take it anymore.

Healthy hate defines what you no longer want to be part of. It can be necessary to experience healthy hate to finally decide that you are done with something. When you hit the emotional place where you know that you just can't tolerate something anymore, you will be at the precipice of a breakthrough in your life and will enter a new territory of living abundantly. You can use your hate productively in order to take care of yourself, set boundaries, and make constructive changes. You can decide that you will not be part of abusive relationships anymore and start to weed the toxic people out of your life. If you can't get them completely out of your life, you may at least be able to distance yourself from them significantly to the point where they don't really affect you anymore.

In order to break out of the victim mentality, you need to recognize and understand your own suffering. This can take time and often requires help from others, but it is well worth the effort and work to get there. You also need someone else to witness your suffering. Validation from another person solidifies your feelings and perceptions and helps you believe in yourself, your inner guidance, and intuition. While you once may have wondered whether you were crazy, with validation from another trusted person, you will not. By having your suffering witnessed and validated, you will know it is real, and you will know that you are not alone. Once you understand your suffering, and someone else also understands it, it is easier to move on. Understanding your suffering is important, and once that happens, you don't need to stay there.

If you had a depressed or disempowered parent, you may be more vulnerable to the victim mentality due to the negative role modeling. One important piece of letting go of the victim identity is to recognize that you are defined by yourself and not by others. You have the ability, strength, and power to redefine yourself at any point in your life. Just because you have behaved or thought like a victim for a long time does not mean that you can't change now.

Just like you can change your physical self through diet and exercise, you can change your mindset through educating yourself, cultivating support, making new choices, and committing to a new way of thinking. Once you change your thinking, everything flows from there. All you need to do to begin is decide that you are not going to be a victim anymore.

Another aspect of moving out of the victim mentality involves moving from scarcity thinking to abundance thinking. In a scarcity mentality, we believe that there is not enough of anything in the world and that we will not be taken care of or given our fair share of what we need in life. We see the world as a place that is scarce in resources. We believe that there is not enough to go around. This can make us feel chronically fearful and victimized, always believing that there is not enough and that we will never have enough.

In an abundance mentality, we believe there is plenty of everything in the world. There are plenty of resources: spiritually, materially, financially. There is enough time, money, and love to go around. With an abundance mentality, you know that there is always more and that you will always be given more. You have a basic trust in the universe that your needs will be met and that you will be taken care of.

With this mentality, you don't feel like a victim, because you trust that more good things are around the corner and that all will be well. If you never had enough money, love, or attention, it is easy to believe that that's the way that life is always going to be. Recognizing the abundance in the universe can be very freeing and empowering. You can make the decision to change your thinking and remind yourself that all is well.

Once you make this decision, you can do the internal psychological work to understand your core beliefs and thought patterns. This is the first step that will allow you to begin to change them. When you change your thinking, you change everything in your life. Once you change, you will never permanently go back to the way you were before. You might have small lapses from time to time when you fall back into old thinking, but you will be able to more easily extricate yourself from them. The lapses will become shorter and further apart. Eventually, you will realize that you have become a new person. It may take a long time for all of this significant and profound change to occur, but you can start today.

7

DEVELOPING SELF WORTH

This is the point at which you start taking back your power. You had it all along, but you didn't know how to access it and use it. Now it is time for you to claim what is yours – your self-esteem and self-worth. When you work on building yourself up from the inside, you will not be easily shaken again. Once you have faced your trauma, there is only one way to go, and that is up. The strongest people are not those who have never had a problem but rather those who have been through a lot of difficulty and come through it. You will become strong in the broken places.

Through learning and practicing a new set of skills and behaviors, you will develop the capacity to face the past, handle difficult and abusive people in the present, and take care of yourself in all situations. Although you may never be able to trust everyone, you will always trust yourself to take care of yourself. You will come to know that although you might get rattled, you will never be completely shaken to pieces. You will always learn, grow, and come out stronger on the other side.

At first, practicing new behaviors may feel awkward and uncomfortable. You might find yourself going from one extreme and then going too far the other way. Don't worry; the pendulum always come back to find its balance in the middle. If you have a history of never speaking up for yourself, you might find it awkward to do so. You might come on too strong in the beginning, but you will eventually learn how to handle situations in the most adaptive way. Trial and error will teach you a lot about what works for you. You will also learn that you are stronger in some areas and need more work in others.

The areas that you need to work on will continually be presented to you by your life situations. You will repeatedly be given the lessons that you need in order to grow stronger. If you feel like you didn't pass a test or that you didn't handle a particular situation very well, don't worry. It often takes several attempts at doing something differently in order to succeed. Most people require at least a few tries before a new behavior really works out and sticks with them. There is no loss in not succeeding the first time or not doing something perfectly; the only failure is to not try at all.

Here are some of the most effective strategies that you can use to develop self -worth:

FIND YOUR VOICE

One of the first steps to developing self-worth is finding your voice. Start talking about your story and sharing more about who you are and what you have gone through. You may have been conditioned in a dysfunctional family not to talk about anything personal or embarrassing and not to share things that might make the family look bad. Not talking is what fosters secrecy and shame, and finding your voice is the antidote. Once you start talking to healthy people who do not shame you, you will realize that you never had anything to be ashamed of in the first place. You are just a normal human being going through the pains of growing up in dysfunction like so many others. It takes a while to learn how to use your voice.

In the beginning, it may feel very awkward to you, and you may not feel like you know how to do it. Just start with whatever comes to mind and take it from there. As you begin to find your voice, talking will become easier for you. If you are in a group setting where you can listen to others, it will be even more productive in helping you to learn to communicate well. When we talk about what is going on inside of us, we release it from our being, and we become free. Whatever we don't talk about we tend to act out in our lives.

One of the most valuable aspects of psychotherapy is having a forum where you can talk things out in a safe setting without having to act them out in your life. When we are able to talk, we are much less likely to unconsciously act out in destructive ways.

When it comes to communicating, there is a difference between talking and really saying something. The more that you talk, the more you will learn how to focus on what's really important and communicate your truth. Express yourself freely without fear of other people's reactions to what you are saying. It is through honestly communicating our truth that we are set free from what has been locked inside of us. Practice using your voice even when you don't feel like it. Your communication skills will continue to improve, and eventually you will be able to say a lot more than you thought you were capable of. You will find your voice. Give yourself a chance, open up, and talk.

TRUST

Trust can be very difficult for people who have experienced emotional trauma. You may have been traumatized by the people you trusted the most and learned that it is not safe to trust. As a child, you didn't have much choice about who was in your world. Other than school and neighborhood friends, the people in your primary family were the ones that you were around the most. If they were not trustworthy, why would you trust anyone else?

We can learn to trust trustworthy people. The way that we know that someone is trustworthy is by getting to know them over time and assessing whether they are consistent, respectful, and kind in their interactions with us. If our experiences with them are consistently good, and their behavior is healthy, we can begin to trust them. We can start by opening up slowly and then gradually opening up more as the relationship deepens and grows.

Healthy relationships evolve slowly. Anything that feels too quick or intense is probably not healthy. Allow yourself time to get to know people and give them a chance. Most people's hearts are in the right place, and they want friends too. By simply being honest, intimacy with others grows. Remember that if you see red flags, you can always take a step backwards. But if a relationship feels good, keep moving forward, and build a new connection in your life. There are safe and healthy people whom you can trust. The healthier you become, the more you are going to draw healthier people towards you. Water tends to seek its own level, and we tend to find people who we match up with. Keep on investing in your own growth, and healthier people will be drawn to you.

LISTEN

Listening is an important part of the recovery process. There are many ways to listen, including spending quiet time in meditation – a time when you listen to God or the universe – listening to your inner self, or listening to others. By listening and hearing what we need to hear at the exact moment that we need to hear it, our consciousness can shift in an instant. We can have small or large awakenings, depending on what we are ready to experience in our growth.

Sometimes we may discount certain people because we believe that they don't have anything to offer us. While this may be true in some cases, we can often be surprised by where our lessons come from.

It is important to keep an open mind and heart and listen for guidance from all places. Groups are particularly rich in what they offer, because you can hear many different people talking about a subject, and you have much wisdom to draw from. Sometimes we even receive important messages from unexpected places like a movie or a song. Stay open, put yourself in healthy environments, listen, and see what happens.

FEEL

Allow yourself to feel. This means allowing yourself to have all of your feelings: good and bad, light and dark. Embrace all parts of yourself. We cannot permit certain feelings and deny others. We have to allow all of them. If we don't do that, we will become fragmented, and our disavowed feelings will become split off and trapped inside of us, causing us to become unhealthy and imbalanced. But allowing ourselves to have our feelings can be a very difficult thing to do.

Allowing ourselves to feel grief is perhaps the most critical component of healing and emotional freedom. It is the stored grief resulting from past trauma that fuels most of our current dysfunction, addictions, and emotional problems. When we allow ourselves to access and feel grief, we are cleansed at the deepest level. Our grief is our core pain, and accepting and feeling it is our ticket out of emotional trauma.

Many of us were shut down by dysfunctional families who told us that certain feelings were okay and others were not. We learned to compartmentalize, presenting a mask to the world and only allowing ourselves to express the feelings we thought were acceptable. Until we are able to allow and express all of our feelings in a healthy way, it is difficult to feel whole and integrated. We cannot compartmentalize our feelings and our lives. We need to seek healthy integration both within ourselves and externally in our lives. If someone is healthy for you, they will accept you as you are and allow you to have all of your feelings.

One way that you will know if you are with someone who is safe is by whether or not you can cry with them. If you can cry with someone, then you probably feel safe with them. It takes a fair amount of trust to be able to get to that depth of emotion and allow yourself to release it. Many people feel that crying is a bad thing, but it is actually very healthy. It is like a spiritual cleansing of the soul and the central nervous system. It allows us to recalibrate our emotional thermostat and rebalance the things that are a little bit out of whack. Sometimes a good cry can completely refresh you and purge you of old pain that you have been carrying for a long time.

As you start to feel more of your feelings, you might find that you experience waves of tears from time to time. This can be very healthy. It can happen randomly out of the blue, be caused by specific situations, or even occur unexpectedly when you are still. We often have to slow down and be quiet enough to allow our deeper feelings to surface.

This means that we also need to put a stop to our addictive and compulsive behaviors that distract us from our feelings. When we let go of these compulsions, the feelings come up. Your job is simply to feel them and be with them. Remember that feelings have a beginning, a middle, and an end. Allow yourself to feel and ride the roller coaster until it stops. You will get to the other side.

Once you learn how to be with your feelings and sit with yourself, you will have come a long way in your healing process. This is one of the hardest things to do, because we often feel like our feelings are going to kill us. They never do; they only feel like they will. Every single feeling that you have ever had has changed and passed. No matter what feelings come up for you, just allow them, embrace them, and be with yourself.

REMEMBER

Emotional trauma can make you not want to remember. There is a tendency to try to sweep things under the rug, put them in the past, and try to move on. But in doing this, we bury our feelings alive. They do not die. They just stay inside of us, waiting to get out. We need to remember what has happened, one piece at a time. The people in your life who traumatized you will not want you to do this, so you probably don't want to discuss your trauma with them unless they have become healthy and safe people. You will want to remember your own story as best you can with safe people, and it will probably come back to you very slowly, one bit at a time.

You may experience memory bubbles once you are engaged in healing from trauma. Memory bubbles are when discrete memories will bubble up from your unconscious into your consciousness at unexpected times. This is part of the healing process and is a sign that you are getting well. Each memory that bubbles up to the surface is like a dot in the interconnected story of your life. The more dots you have, the more dots you can connect. At some point, you will be able to connect the dots very clearly and understand your whole life and your story as you never have done before.

In order to connect the dots, we must first remember. We must remember what happened, what didn't happen, and what we missed out on. Part of trauma is the abuse that you experienced and another part has to do with your unmet needs - the things that did not happen and never will. We can experience intense feelings of grief around both of these. Don't be afraid of grief, just allow yourself to remember and to have the feelings around what you remember. The more you try to remember, the more you will be able to remember, and your story will eventually make more sense to you.

Many people who have experienced emotional trauma have a vague sense of mystery about certain parts of their childhood or their life. These blind spots will eventually come to light, and you will be able to see your history in a new way, with yourself at the center. You will be able to understand yourself at a much deeper level and make sense of the things that you do in the present. There are always reasons for why we do what we do and persist in our behaviors. Once you understand the story behind you, you will be able to understand yourself more deeply, write a new story, and choose to become the best version of yourself.

ASSERTIVENESS

Although other people may have dismissed you or shut you down in the past, you can learn to assert yourself appropriately. It is not rude or distasteful to be assertive; it is what healthy adults do. By being assertive, you are behaving like a grown up. Being passive is childlike and often leads to depression. When you assert yourself, you stand for yourself, not against others.

You may have grown up in a family system where expressing yourself was discouraged, but you are no longer a child, and you have the right to express and assert yourself as any other adult does. You don't need to be afraid to speak up. If someone else doesn't like what you have to say, that is okay. What is important is that you speak up, honor your truth, and take care of yourself when you need to.

There are times when you can just let things go, and you don't need to speak up. But there are other times when it is important to stand up for yourself. Very often, people are pleasantly surprised when they first start doing this because others don't fight back. They simply accept what you are saying, and they understand. Most people in the world are reasonable, and if you stand up for yourself, they will accept it. And if they don't, you've still done the right thing. Others will just have to learn to deal with it.

If you grew up with emotional trauma, it

might not feel safe to behave like an adult and stand up for yourself. If you were around abusive people who bullied you, tormented you, shut you down, or were mean, you might feel too anxious to do it. But even if you feel like it's not worth the effort, it is.

If you are around an abusive person, it is even more important that you speak up for yourself and be assertive. Very often, a bully will back down if you stand up to them. But if you don't stand up to them, they will walk all over you.

Either way, standing up for yourself when you need to is always the right thing to do. And in the worst-case scenario, if someone disagrees and is abusive towards you, you can simply walk away. It is much easier to walk away in peace after you have stated your truth. It will take up much less room in your head if you have said what you need to say. Speaking up can give you closure and help you to let go. Once you do your part, and it is on them.

SETTING BOUNDARIES

Setting boundaries is one of the greatest gifts we can give ourselves. It means knowing our limits and sticking to them regardless of what other people do. Our boundaries are about what we can or cannot do, what we will or will not accept, what we will or will not tolerate, and how much we will or will not give. Boundaries are not about telling another person what to do or about controlling them; rather, they are about stating our own limits both to ourselves and to others.

Boundaries are truly the key to sanity when dealing with difficult people. Portion control is an effective technique to use around toxic people. Sometimes, the unhealthiest people that we know are in our own families, and we have to see them regularly. If we are able to set boundaries and use portion control in dealing with them, we can manage these relationships in a way that works for us.

You get to decide how much of a person you can handle. Just like with food, you need portions and balance. The same principle applies in relationships. If you can be with a difficult person for no more than two hours, plan something where you meet in neutral place, have your own transportation, and are able to leave after two hours. Then stick to the schedule you have decided will work for you.

Is not up to other people to set your boundaries. That is your responsibility. What do you do if people don't respect your boundaries? You respect those boundaries anyway. This means that you decide what will work for you, and you do that. Only you can decide how much of something is good for you, and it is your responsibility to be honest with yourself about it and to set appropriate boundaries for yourself. This is a critical aspect of self-care.

Some people will really try to push your boundaries and try to get their own way. When this happens, don't let yourself be pushed around. Simply say what you mean, mean what you say, and don't say it meanly. State your boundary in a matter-of-fact tone of voice, without emotion, almost in a businesslike fashion. If someone continues to question you and tries to push you around, restate your boundaries. Just use the broken record technique as much as you need to until they get it. If they don't get it, walk away in peace when you feel that you have done all you can do.

KNOW WHEN TO WALK AWAY

How do you know when it's time to walk away? When you can't stand it anymore. When you feel like you've done all you can do, and you don't want to waste anymore of your precious time and energy on a person.

When your dignity becomes more important than the relationship. When you have handed your power over to someone, and you have decided that it's time to take it back. When you feel done.

When it is time to walk away from someone, you will know. You won't have to try and guess whether it is time to walk away. Once you know that it is time to walk away, turn and don't look back. This is time to end all contact with that person for as long as you need to. Sometimes, the only way to get someone off your mind and out of your soul is to go no contact. Abstinence really does work.

If you are in a toxic or addictive relationship, the dysfunction can persist for years when the abusive partner continues to toss you crumbs from time to time. You have to ask yourself if you deserve only crumbs and if you are willing to settle for them. If not, cut your losses, and walk away.

In a toxic relationship, the other person is probably not going to change, especially if they are a narcissist. People who have experienced emotional trauma are particularly vulnerable to being attracted to narcissists. And narcissists have a way of knowing how to prey on empathic people who will feed their ego-driven needs. If you have ever been in a relationship with a narcissist, you know what it's like to be in constant pain and to have your soul literally sucked out of your being. Once you get it back, you don't ever want to give it up again. The only way to make sure that this spiritual vampire doesn't suck the life out of you again is to walk away and stay away. Claim your own power instead of giving it away.

IF YOU CAN'T WALK AWAY

Walking away is easier in some situations than it is in others. With acquaintances and casual relationships, it is very easy to simply pick up your toys and go home. However, when you are married to a toxic person, or they are in your family, it is much harder to walk away permanently. When people are built into your family life, you may only be able to walk away temporarily. But that can be good enough to help you to regain your balance. Minimize contact, be respectful, stand up for yourself, call them out on their bad behavior, and keep as much distance as you can. If you change your behavior, the dynamic will change.

It only takes one person to change a relationship, and that person can be you. If you change your outlook and your behaviors, the whole relationship dynamic will change, even if the other person does nothing differently. You have enormous power to create change just by altering the course of your own behavior. Usually, if one changes, the other one will also go through some changes. But don't focus on them. Just focus on changing yourself, and trust that things will work out in the end.

CULTIVATE A SUPPORT SYSTEM

In order to heal from emotional trauma, you will need to work on yourself for a period. In order to do this, you will need to have a strong support system. Healing cannot be done as effectively alone. Reading self-help books can be extremely beneficial, but reading a book by yourself is usually not enough to transform yourself and experience profound and lasting healing.

To heal, we need other people. Look for healthy people to support you. Some of the following resources can be very helpful: a therapist, a spiritual advisor, friends, family, a church community, spiritual centers, and 12 step programs. There is a vast world of resources and healing out there, and there are many people who will be able to help you if you reach out. It is your responsibility to do the reaching out, because resources are not going to come to you. The more tools that you have in your support system, the deeper and more quickly you will heal. Go out and find as much help as you can, and use it regularly. It will become a very healthy replacement for the dysfunction that you had in your life before, and you will find yourself slowly, but surely, healing and experiencing an inner transformation.

SELF-CARE

Self-care is the bedrock of self-esteem. Your most important job each and every day is to take good care of yourself physically, emotionally, and spiritually. The four cornerstones of self-care are sleep, exercise, nutrition, and mental health care. Many people who have experienced emotional trauma struggle with the basics of self-care, including being able to sleep and relax. Although everyone's needs for sleep are individual, is important that you know what you need and make sure that you allow yourself the time to have it. This may include a winding down period at the end of the day before bedtime and period of quiet reflection after you wake up.

Cultivate a morning routine. This is one

of the most valuable tools that you can have. Practicing a regular morning routine sets the tone for the day and fosters emotional and physical self-regulation. Meditation, prayer, reading, journaling, stretching, exercise, and having a healthy breakfast are enormously helpful in getting the day off to a good start. Even if you cannot make time for all of your routine in the morning, try to find creative ways to incorporate it into your life.

Find time to exercise regularly, and pay attention to what you eat. Too many people eat mindlessly and feed on "food-like" substances that have very little nutrition. Make sure that whatever you eat is nutritionally healthy and actually nourishes your body and gives you energy.

Mental health care is a fundamental activity that will keep you on track. This can involve seeing a therapist or psychiatrist, taking medication if needed, participating in supportive 12 step groups, speaking with a spiritual advisor or other mentor, and cultivating other spiritual, cultural, or artistic communities. We all have a basic need to be part of community, and this is true at any age. Although we continue to get older, in some ways we don't really change all that much.

AUTHENTICITY

The journey towards freedom and self-worth is paved with cultivating authenticity. Authenticity involves being who you truly are and shedding false masks worn to gain acceptance and approval in the world. Really being yourself is perhaps the most important thing you will ever do. If people don't know who you really are, how can you give them all you've got?

Emotional trauma can make you feel afraid of being yourself. It can make you feel like you have to twist yourself into a pretzel in order to be what you think other people want you to be. This is often learned early on in life when we tried to soothe the unstable people around us and keep them from acting out. But we don't have to do that; we are free to be who we really are.

Honesty is the key to becoming more authentic. As you start to become more comfortable with who you are, you will be more able to honestly say what you think, feel, need, and want. You will respond honestly to other people's communications with you. You will let go of the need to control their reactions, and simply be who you are. Although you may feel uncomfortably vulnerable at first, it will get easier with time and practice. Eventually, you will come to a point where living in your false self no longer feels comfortable. You will become unable to be anything other than who you really are. And you will feel confident in that person, because you will know that you are fully being yourself.

MEDITATION AND MINDFULNESS

Cultivate a regular meditation practice. Of all the things that you can do for your well-being, meditation is one of the most powerful. A simple way to begin your meditation practice is to do the following: when you wake up in the morning, take 10-15 minutes to sit quietly, close your eyes, and focus on your breathing. Count your exhales from one to ten, and then do that over and over again. When your mind wanders, which it will, recognize that you have moved into thinking mode, and gently bring yourself back to counting. Even the most experienced meditators have wandering minds, so this doesn't mean that you have failed. Each time your mind wanders, just go back to counting, relax, and breathe.

When you first begin to meditate, you may only be able to sit for a couple minutes. This is perfectly fine. Just do what feels natural, relax, and let your meditation practice grow and evolve in a gentle and natural fashion. Most people naturally want to do a little more as they get used to it. If you work up to twelve minutes, you will have received the maximum benefit for your brain. And if you do this in the morning, you will carry the benefits with you throughout the entire day, leaving you with a sense of peace, calm, and non-reactivity that will grow over time.

Another benefit of meditating is that you become more attuned to the present moment, automatically practice mindfulness, and develop a growing capacity to focus on one thing at a time. Being able to focus on one thing at a time allows you increase your effectiveness in every area of your life. Meditation is one of the most effective tools for self-regulation. It fosters stability and allows you to reset yourself each and every day.

EVALUATE YOUR STANDARDS

When you have lived with emotional trauma, your self-esteem really takes a beating. You start accepting less than what you really want because it feels like that's all you can get. You can fall into a pattern of settling for very little instead of living to your full potential. If you find yourself in relationships where you're doing all the giving and your needs are not really being met, ask yourself why you are settling for crumbs. Do you believe that this is the best you can do? Do you feel like there's not much out there and you'd better take what you can? Do you have little faith that the world is an abundant place and will continue to provide what you need? Go for what you really want instead of settling for less.

GIVE TO OTHERS

One of the most powerful acts of self-esteem is to find a way to give back and help others. One of the most meaningful tasks in life in is finding a way to leave the world a little better than you found it. There are millions of ways that you can help people, and whatever you choose to do, let it be something that you enjoy.

Remember that all the challenges that you have experience can serve a purpose. Whatever you have gone through and mastered in your life you can share with other people and give them strength to do the same. We can do service on both a small and large scale depending on the opportunities that present themselves and the time we have available to do it.

One important aspect of helping others is that it can be very healing for you to give the very thing that you never received. For example, if your parents were never there for you, it can be a healing experience to be there fully for your children or stepchildren and become the parent you always wish you had. It is possible for us to heal our wounds by paying forward what we have missed out on. While it may seem counterintuitive, it works. When you give other people the things that you have always wanted for yourself, a lot of abundance comes back towards you. Find a way to help somebody every single day, whether it is as small as giving a compliment or performing an act of service to someone in need.

What matters most is that there is some portion of your life where you give to others in a way that is meaningful to you. This will build up your feeling of self- worth, because you will see yourself as a person of abundance who has enough and who has something of value to offer others. When you see yourself as valuable, you will feel better, and you will help another person. It's a win-win situation.

Regardless of how little you think you have to give, give what you can to others; just make sure that you are not giving at your own expense. Give from your bounty and not your reserve. This can be part of your profession, or it can be something you do on the side in your free time. Regardless of how you do it, recognize that in giving, the giver receives even more than the receiver.

LEARN TO ENJOY YOUR OWN COMPANY

Learning to enjoy your own company is an important part of growing your self-esteem and sense of self-worth. You do not have to be dependent upon others to enjoy your time and activities. While it is wonderful to share experiences with other people, it is not always a necessity. Sometimes there is no one around to do things with you. Does this mean that you have to sit around and feel sorry for yourself? Not at all. You can learn to cherish your time to yourself, whether you are engaged in quiet reflection or in activities that you love. You can go out to eat at a nice restaurant by yourself or go to a movie, a concert, or a museum and have an absolutely wonderful time. Learning to enjoy your time alone is an important part of maturity, self-acceptance, and personal growth.

You are responsible for making the most of and enjoying all of your time. It doesn't have to depend on anyone else, not even on your life partner. Remember that your partner is not your property. There are going to be times when the two of you have very different ideas about what you want to do, and you may need to give each other the space to do it. Become your own best friend, and you will never feel lonely.

While being alone is one thing, feeling lonely while you're doing it is another. Time to yourself is a time to connect with yourself, with activities, or with a higher power. It is a time of active connection. Being lonely is about feeling disconnected, and that is a completely different issue.

If you are connected to yourself most of the time, you are unlikely to feel lonely. You will know that regardless of who you are with, you can always be in good company with yourself. You will also start to realize that it is preferable to be alone with yourself rather than with someone who drags you down, puts you down, criticizes you, is negative, or is just plain bad to be with. You don't need to be with people out of desperation just to avoid being alone. Recognize that no matter what, you've always got yourself, and that is enough.

CHOICES

Remember that you always have choices. Just because you have made a particular choice for a long time doesn't mean that you can't start making different choices. People might not like it at first, but they will get used to it when you start living as your true self. No one can stop you from taking care of yourself unless you allow them to. It's up to you to continuously take stock of who you are and what is happening in your life and to make adjustments as needed.

We're not supposed to stay the same throughout our lives. We are meant to grow and evolve and become a better version of ourselves. The best way to do this is to continue to small incremental improvements in everything that you do. A daily practice of self-examination will reveal where you might have gone slightly off course and what you need to do to get back on track. No one can make your choices for you; only you can do that for yourself. So, claim your power, take responsibility for yourself, and start making choices that will improve the quality of your life.

REWRITE YOUR OWN STORY

While you can never go back and change the past, you can change the way that you look at your past. You can either look at yourself as a victim or you can look at your past challenges as stepping stones on your journey of growth. You are the author of your own story, and you can create a new story anytime you decide to. One key to this is to create good memories and experiences in the present. The changes that you start making today will create the beginning of a new story. It is never too late to change your attitude or your actions. Even with difficult relationships, by changing yourself, you can change the dynamics and change the way that those relationships play out. The important thing is that you feel good about the life you have lived, the choices you have made, and your own part in your life and your relationships.

BREAKTHROUGH

Recognize when you have had a breakthrough. Very often, a breakthrough doesn't look like one; it looks more like a dead end. When you think you are at a dead end, you can feel depressed and hopeless. You might think there is nothing you can do about your situation. This can actually be a form of surrender in which you come to the end of your old road and start a new one.

Sometimes it can take a long time to ride out the old road. If things feel like they're getting worse and worse, you may be approaching a dead end, which really means that you are approaching a breakthrough.

It is very difficult for human beings to make major changes in a swift and clean way without experiencing setbacks. More often, changes happen through long periods of spiraling, hitting some sort of an emotional bottom, and then swinging upward over a long and slow period. Just as the seasons of weather change slowly, the seasons of our lives also change slowly. But there are certain points in time when we can actually feel that we have had a breakthrough. This is when your consciousness shifts, and you are suddenly able to put things together in a new way and make sense out of your life. You will feel a profound sense that you are headed somewhere good, and you will start to feel hopeful again. If times are tough right now, ride it out until you reach your breakthrough. It will come.

CHOOSE FAITH

With every challenge we encounter, we can either choose the path of fear or the

HOW TO HEAL EMOTIONAL TRAUMA

path of faith. If you have had many difficult experiences in your life, and you are carrying emotional trauma, you may naturally gravitate towards fear. But always remember that fear is not the only choice that you have. When you are controlled by fear, it is not always easy to know what is true and what is false.

Every time you feel fear, you can either feed that fear or feed your faith. You do not have to be a religious person in order to cultivate an attitude of faith. Faith is a choice that we make based on a positive expectation of the future. One way to do this is to look back on earlier experiences in your life. When you recognize times in the past when you felt fearful and things worked out, draw upon this reservoir of experience to cultivate more faith in the future. If things worked out for you in the past, why wouldn't they work out again? Chances are that you have already been through many things that you didn't think you could get through and have come out stronger on the other side.

You can also cultivate faith by talking to supportive people and borrowing their faith. It is important to stay away from naysayers and negative people when you are afraid, because they will only feed your fear. Surround yourself with positive and uplifting people, and their faith will strengthen your faith.

You can also pray to a power greater than yourself in order to draw strength from the divine. Part of life is learning to live with some uncertainty. There are some things that we will never be able to understand or figure out and some things that will never be resolved. When we can accept this, we can move forward in faith, and expect good things to happen. Very often, what we look for and expect is exactly what we will find.

GRATITUDE

Cultivate an active practice of gratitude. Make the choice each day to focus on what you are grateful for. It can be as simple as the fact that you can breathe freely or that you have two feet that allow you to walk. The earlier in the day that you make this choice, the more you will benefit. Remember that whatever we do in the early hours upon awakening sets our emotional thermostat for the day. Choose to fill your mind with positive messages as early in the day as you can. You can do this by reading daily meditation books, listening to speakers through podcasts, attending spiritual groups, or watching something uplifting.

Taking constructive actions will crowd

out negative thinking and get your day off to a good start. Gratitude is one of the most powerful weapons that we have against our own negativity - including fear, anxiety, anger, self-pity, and resentment. Since it is not possible to think two thoughts at the same time, you can interrupt negativity by choosing instead to focus on something that you are grateful for. You can make a gratitude list each day, think grateful thoughts throughout the day, and speak words of gratitude in your interactions with other people. Gratitude is one of the most powerful forces in reshaping our emotional landscape. Use it daily as part of good mental hygiene.

TRUST YOURSELF

You can learn to trust yourself and your ability to make good choices. You don't have to be perfect all the time, and you will make mistakes, but you can trust yourself to know how to take care of yourself when you need to make course corrections. Being loving towards yourself involves gentleness. You can cultivate an attitude of gentleness towards yourself and others. For example, if you make a mistake, you can say to yourself, "Well, that didn't go so well this time. I think I'll do it differently next time."

Give yourself a break and allow yourself to be a human being and learn as you go. A part of maturity and self-worth involves allowing yourself to step out and try new things. If you try something, and it doesn't work, don't worry about it. Trust that you will be guided intuitively from within and that you will know what to do and where to go next. Mistakes are part of life, and we often learn the most important lessons from our mistakes. Once you know that you're capable of taking care of yourself even when you've gone sideways, you will trust that you can always get yourself back on course. Knowing that you can take care of yourself under all conditions is one of the great gifts of healing.

Remember that adversity can give us enormous gifts. Everything happens for a reason, and it is your job to make lemonade out of lemons. Adversity can create resilience in a way that nothing else can. By being tested to our limits, we grow in our capacity to endure the pain of life and turn it into something positive that we can use to help ourselves and others.

If you have been through emotional trauma, you have learned to endure a lot of pain. This creates positive character traits

such as patience, tolerance, sensitivity, compassion, endurance, and self-control. As diamonds are made under pressure, so are we. Many of our strongest and most valuable traits are the result of the greatest challenges in our life. When we learn to overcome those challenges, we become remade and made into a better version of ourselves. It is through difficulty and the cracks in life that the light can come in. The most difficult situations can bring the brightest light into your life. Look to the light and keep walking towards it. Let the light come in, and let your own light shine out onto others. The darker it has been for you, the brighter your light is going to be. So shine on, and be all that you were meant to be.

ABOUT THE AUTHOR

Dr. Anita Gadhia-Smith, author of four other books, is a psychotherapist in Washington, D.C. specializing in addictions, recovery, and relationship issues. She is particularly effective, discerning and insightful about current issues that have a psychological impact on individuals and couples. She has served as a consultant to the United States Congress in parity legislation for substance abuse treatment. She has also spoken nationally and internationally on radio, television, and other media as an expert on a variety of topical subjects.

One of the things that distinguishes Dr. Anita Gadhia-Smith is her own personal history of addiction as well as over two decades of recovery. She has had a first-hand experience of a spiritual, physical and emotional "bottoming out" followed by a remarkable story of recovery and commitment to helping others who suffer with alcoholism, addictions and relationship issues. Her history and training allow her to approach her work, her perspective and her writing as a "healed healer." Her story is one of redemption – she is a unique therapist who has become a successful, self-actualized woman by way of an intense struggle and personal journey in her own right. Her insights and wisdom are tremendous – and inspiring – about how to obtain and maintain ongoing balance in our lives. Dr. Gadhia-Smith's other bestselling books, "FROM ADDICTION TO RECOVERY," "PRACTICAL THERAPY," "LIVE AND LOVE EACH DAY," and "HOW TO STAY TOGETHER" are available on Amazon.com.

Dr. Gadhia-Smith earned her undergraduate degree from The Johns Hopkins University (BA, 1985) and graduate degrees from The Catholic University of America (MSW, 1999) and Southern California University, (PSYD, 2001). In her private practice in Washington, D.C., Dr. Gadhia-Smith works with adults and adolescents in individual, couple, and family modalities and says, "Therapy is a journey through which we find our authentic selves and become the best we can be. Through therapy, profound and lasting change can occur. My approach is to meet you where you are and to help you to move towards your goals, overcome obstacles and achieve maximum growth."

Awarded "Best of Washington DC, Psychotherapy, 2013 and 2018" by the Washington DC Award Program. Honored as Professional of the Year in Psychotherapy by Strathmore's Who's Who Publication, 2013-2014. Visit her website at www.practicaltherapy.net.

Dr. Anita Gadhia-Smith
practicaltherapy.net